Dedication

He knows nothing and he thinks he knows everything. That points clearly to a political career.

■ George Bernard Shaw, in his play *Major Barbara*

There are three sorts of people in the world: the low people, the middle people, and the high people. The low people and the high people are alike in one thing: they have no scruples, no morality. The low are beneath morality, the high are above it. …

It is the middle people who are dangerous: they have both knowledge and purpose. But they, too, have their weak point. They are full of scruples: chained hand and foot by their morality and respectability.

■ George Bernard Shaw, in his play *The Man of Destiny*

I love the poorly educated! Yes, I really love the poorly educated.

■ Donald Trump, campaigning for President

This book is dedicated to the scrupulous, moral, and respectable "middle people" of the United States of America – who are engaged in an epic struggle against a "high person" who has proven that he has massive support among the "low people".

Table of Contents

1 – A Haven for White-Collar Crime

If Donald Trump is elected President of the United States on November 8, 2016, the blame should fall squarely on the police, the prosecutors, and especially the judges of Canada – who had a chance to prosecute him in a case that would have proved conclusively to American voters that Mr. Trump is unfit for the most powerful position in the world.

If Canada were not such a haven for large-scale deception and falsehood by executives and their corporations, it is this author's well-considered opinion that Donald Trump should be on trial now in Toronto for fraud, facing a minimum sentence of two years in a Canadian prison – and likely much more, given that 50 investors each lost about C$200,000 because they fell for his pitch to invest in **"a bond you can sleep in"** that was – as *proven in court* – an investment that could not possibly earn a profit.

Indeed, buying a hotel suite in Trump's Toronto project was certain to be a liability that is large enough to destroy a middle-class family's financial security.

The case of the Trump International Hotel in Toronto proves two things that matter to all American voters:

- Donald Trump cannot be believed or trusted when he promises to apply his business skills to help ordinary citizens to get ahead; and

- Donald Trump cannot be relied upon to choose qualified, properly-experienced, and honest executives to run the federal government of the United States of America.

Donald Trump took advantage of Canada's accommodation of large-scale white-collar crime to make money on the backs of

3

inexperienced investors in Toronto. He used his reputation as a successful developer and operator of hotels to deceive vulnerable people into buying condominiums as investments that were certain to be losing propositions.

The proof is absolute – and damning – because a credible Canadian judge (who has no racial, religious, or ethnic status that might taint his impartiality in Mr. Trump's eyes) applied Canada's "buyer beware" judicial policy to totally exonerate Mr. Trump *personally* in a civil lawsuit brought by two of the victims – while at the same time fully exposing the fraudulent nature of the investment in the hotel-condo units that Mr. Trump himself was promoting to unsophisticated investors.

For readers who have limited time, the most significant facts are in Chapter 4, which summarizes the 48-page decision issued on July 10, 2015.

Donald Trump's deceit and falsehoods

Donald Trump's falsehoods were extensively advertised. Trump's deceptive sales pitches and impossible promises were widely disseminated on YouTube. The evidence against Donald Trump personally is overwhelming.

Every potential purchaser who ventured into the Toronto sales office was given promotional literature featuring Donald Trump, along with a customized Estimated Return on Investment that no investor could ever actually realize.

What Trump, his sales associates, and development partners executed fell solidly within the definition of fraud in the Criminal Code of Canada (see Chapter 6, page 40), and should have resulted in a trial where all of the evidence would be considered openly to determine if Donald Trump should bear personal responsibility for convincing naïve investors to take a high risk that was certain to fail – particularly because crucial facts about hotel operating costs were either *significantly* understated or not disclosed *at all* until after the investors had committed their precious personal funds.

Sadly, prosecution for large-scale fraud rarely occurs in Canada. Instead of being protected by the police and prosecutors, the vulnerable investors in this case had only one remote possibility of recovering some of their losses – a civil lawsuit. Unfortunately for the victims, that strategy was doomed to fail because of judicial policy in Canada that consistently takes the side of rich, important, and powerful people.

The facts could not be more clear:

The deal that Donald Trump was promoting was based on "deceptive documents" that were "replete with misrepresentations of commission, of omission, and of half-truth" – according to the decision in the Superior Court of the Province of Ontario, issued on July 10, 2015.

Judge Paul Perrell's decision in *Singh v. Trump* is a clear warning to anyone who would elect Donald Trump President of the United States on the basis of his promise to Make America Great Again. His deal in Toronto included so many undisclosed or understated costs and charges that no investor owning one of his hotel suites could possibly earn a profit. Indeed, it put the investors on the hook to pay for continuing losses.

Based on the promises made personally by Donald Trump, the plaintiff investors had put family homes at risk to borrow money to invest in the Trump Toronto Tower. The losses were not just investment losses in the ordinary sense; they were losses that struck at the heart of family security.

The decision in the civil lawsuit is a matter of public record. Anyone can read it by going to a public website:

canlii.org   *case name:* **2015 ONSC 4461**

This is a civil lawsuit brought by Sarbjit Singh and Se Na Lee, two of the 50 Canadian investors who purchased suites in the Trump Toronto Tower – units under condominium ownership – as income properties with rights to participate in the Trump-managed Trump International Hotel.

This 48-page decision shows why and how Canada functions as a haven for white-collar crime. In particular, it shows how Donald Trump profited by *deception* and *falsehood* – the very definition of fraud in the Criminal Code of Canada, but fraud is a crime that is rarely prosecuted in Canada against people of stature, such as Mr. Trump.

The lesson for American voters

There are two pillars of the Trump campaign for President of the United States of America: **Fear** and **Money**.

Obviously, Trump's attacks on Mexicans and Muslims are stoking fear and inflaming intolerance on a scale that has not been seen in America since the last gasps of white supremacists resisting the Civil Rights movement of the 1960s. Many competent political analysts and commentators have thoroughly exposed Trump's campaign of Fear. Leading members of his own Republican Party are among the denouncers.

Trump's appeal to Money is a much different matter. It is a sly tactic. Trump drives home the truth that the average American family has not had a real increase in income or accumulated net wealth in about 20 years. He then misleads these victims of capitalism into believing that somehow he can make them *all* rich.

Americans are not foolish enough to believe that *everyone* can be rich, but Trump is encouraging them to believe that he will be able to change the system at least enough that the "smart" voters will be able to profit.

The folly of Trump's appeal to Money is hard to expose in a convincing manner because the majority of American voters have been casualties of the very type of capitalism that has made Trump a rich man. Donald Trump is using a nudge and a wink to convince vulnerable Americans that he will take care of the voters who believe in him – just like he conned naïve investors into buying into the "privilege" of being co-owners of the Trump Toronto Tower.

There are many examples of the bad investments that Trump has sold to Americans and others over this long career as a developer, hotelier, and casino operator. None of these bad deals offer the same clear evidence of fraud as the Toronto project.

For example, the lawsuit by the "students" of Trump University is open to neutralizing arguments on the campaign trail because Donald Trump can display "graduates" who had beneficial experiences despite the obvious flaws in the product they purchased. Indeed, it is possible to develop confidence from the lessons of a confidence man – and confidence is one of the desired outcomes of any program of education. It is certain that some of the "graduates" of Trump University did receive at least some of what they paid for.

Millions of Americans know that capitalism is stacked against them.

At both ends of the political spectrum, they flocked to either the capitalist guru Donald Trump or the socialist dreamer Bernie Sanders because most American families have seen no real improvement in their financial position in two decades.

Whether by accident or design, capitalism in the United States of America under Democrat Bill Clinton and Republican George W. Bush deteriorated into a system by which the very rich could claim almost all new income and accumulated wealth for themselves – and Democrat Barack Obama has not been able to do anything to restore economic fairness.

Donald Trump played the system that he now attacks as the impediment to rebuilding prosperity for the average American family. He took advantage of immigrants' desperation for any form of work in order to staff his hotels, golf courses, casinos, and other businesses. He did not hesitate to use cheap foreign manufacturers to produce some of his branded products. **He sold investments that enriched himself at the expense of vulnerable victims such as the buyers of his hotel suites in Toronto.**

Trump can be readily denounced for his hypocrisy, but desperate voters will be susceptible to his siren call because he is someone *outside* the political system that has lost the confidence of millions of Americans. His opponent, Hillary Clinton, is open to attack precisely because she has more experience *inside* that system than any Presidential contender in history, and also because she has many flaws in her character and blemishes on her public record.

Trump offends rational citizens to an extent that is unprecedented in U.S. history, but there remains a risk that he can win the election in November because enough Americans are desperate for change.

Will you be better off with Clinton or Trump?

Personal financial impact is the most important factor in most American voters' final decision when they mark their ballots. Americans will be asking themselves in November: Will I and my family be better off with another Clinton as President, or do we need a bold and different approach under Trump?

Thus, no matter how outrageous, divisive, or destructive Trump's rhetoric, there is a chance that he will win in November because so many Americans have lost confidence in the political system, feel cheated by the economy, and are willing to try something new.

The story of the Trump Toronto Tower is a revealing lesson for every American who is thinking of "investing" his or her vote in the business plans of Donald Trump.

Unlike Trump University, there is absolutely no "investor" who made a dime of profit in his Toronto hotel development – and the project was doomed from the beginning because of the unachievable, brazenly-false promises made by Donald John Trump himself, and the lack of honesty and skills in his partners.

His reputation and personal promises were the reasons why investors decided to risk their family assets in his hotel, and Trump's failure to keep those promises is the reason that every one of the 206 investors lost money, and 50 of them were hit with huge losses.

If Mr. Trump truly believed what he says about standing up for the ordinary citizen, he would not have contested the civil lawsuit. Instead, he would have settled with the plaintiffs: He would have refunded the money that middle-class investors had paid for hotel-condo units that could never make a profit. If Donald Trump is as rich as he claims to be, it would be a trifle to buy back those condominium units and operate them himself as hotel suites.

The truth is that he always knew he was selling an outrageously-risky investment – one that he wanted to sell off as quickly as possible. As structured by Donald Trump and his development partners, it could never be "a bond you can sleep in."

9

2 – The Siren Call of Owning Part of a Trump Hotel

It is almost certain that Donald Trump will not release his personal income-tax returns for public scrutiny prior to Election Day. That will make him the first presidential contender in decades who refused to formally and comprehensively reveal his personal financial status.

There are many reasons for this, but the main one is that the hotel business is not nearly as profitable as Trump claims it to be, and thus he is not nearly as rich and successful as he trumpets himself to be. (Donald Trump also relies extensively on golf courses for his income, and golf has become a losing business because of worldwide overcapacity at the same time as golf's popularity has been significantly declining. The casino business is much the same.)

Mr. Trump's tax returns would also be certain to reveal some very aggressive tactics to avoid taxes, which is normal for rich businessmen, but would be eye-opening for voters who might still want to believe that Trump cares about America.

Ever since the internet became a fact of life in the developed world, the hotel business has been a poor investment in at least 95% of locations.

Only where there is high and growing demand for overnight accommodation and significant barriers to entry by new providers – or in premium locations where spectacular views, historic architecture, or hard-to-duplicate facilities provide unique appeal – do hoteliers have any real pricing power.

The internet has empowered individuals to compete on an equal footing with branded hotels. New, small-scale entrants to the overnight accommodation business are able to rely on family labour, have no unions or costly corporate regulation, and are usually subject to substantially lower taxes. These individuals can flood the market with bed-and-breakfasts, private apartments, and small inns at nightly rates that prevent conventional hoteliers from keeping up with the rest of the economy.

The blunt truth is that overnight accommodation has become a routine commodity whose price cannot rise significantly without attracting even more providers into a business that is very easy to enter.

It is impossible to *Make Hotels Great Again!*

There is no small irony in the fact that hoteliers are among the many Americans who haven't had a real raise in pay in more than a decade! Donald Trump will not admit it, but he has been suffering as much as the voters he appeals to. His own core business offers no hope for improvement.

Across America and around the world, owning a hotel is unlikely to return more than 5 or 6% on money invested in the capital assets, while having to endure the risk of significant operating losses during downturns in the business cycle. That is not good enough for a corporation, and does not make Donald Trump fabulously wealthy, as he pretends he is.

Most of the large hotel corporations have been selling off their properties because of the low annual returns on investment. The buyers are most often large institutional investors who want some real estate as a portion of their diversified holdings. Owning the real estate in the form of hotels can be attractive to the long-term strategy of a deep-pocketed pension fund – particularly if the hotel is one of the small minority of properties that have a premium location, a heritage structure, or unique attributes that might generate a significant capital gain in addition to the modest annual return.

The famed Waldorf-Astoria Hotel in Manhattan is a revealing example of what is happening to the hotel industry, even for a property with a superior brand name and a very desirable location. It had already been sold off to an insurance company (based in China), but will be closed in 2017 for a total makeover. A maximum of 500 of the current 1400 hotel suites will remain as part of a much-smaller hotel, while the rest of the space will be converted to residential condos.

The result of the sell-off of real estate across the industry is that most hotel companies are now just agencies that provide branding and management services. They are not interested in owning land, bricks, and mortar, but will happily charge high fees to any owner who will meet their standards for facilities and services in desirable locations.

There *is* one way for developers like Trump to make money

There *is* a way to make money in the business of *developing* hotels, and that is by selling individual hotel suites as condominium units to be professionally managed as a hotel.

A superior location, good design, competent construction, and *honest* management can combine to produce an acceptable long-term investment for small-scale individual investors.

But, it should be only a portion of an investor's portfolio, so that other assets can be drawn upon when the hotel business is in a slow cycle. Under no circumstances should an investor risk the family home as the only source of funding to support the purchase of condo-hotel unit. Trump and his associates took advantage of naïve investors who did not know these essential facts (and the buyers certainly were not told the hard truth or given any other fair warning).

At a time when guaranteed investment certificates are paying a pittance, it can make sense for a small investor with a diversified investment portfolio to buy a piece of real estate – a suite in a condo-hotel – that earns a 5% annual return most years, along with reasonable potential for capital gains.

A condo-hotel looks and functions like a conventional hotel. The difference is that the investors own real estate instead of a share certificate. The value of the real estate, provided that it is properly insured against all perils and there are adequate reserve funds being built up to cover future maintenance, is unlikely to go to zero the way that a share certificate can. It is real estate, after all. Even if an uninsured catastrophe destroyed the building, the land would still be there.

However, the liabilities of owning a condo-hotel unit can be substantial – enough to overwhelm unsophisticated investors who have borrowed too much and cannot afford to cover operating losses, which are certain during the start-up period, and can easily occur during business cycles.

The greatest risk is posed by dishonest or incompetent management.

Using aggressive sales techniques, developers have flocked into the condo-hotel business in the past two decades, and many have given the industry a bad name because they were not honest.

Once the hotel is operating, the profit margin is so thin that management must be absolutely scrupulous in controlling costs and treating the individual owners fairly.

The best-known hotel brands will rarely, if ever, allow a condo-hotel to operate under their banner. Hotel corporations want to deal directly with owners who are deep-pocketed investors; they are not interested in catering to a large number of individual suite owners who are part of a condominium corporation.

Entirely reliant on Donald Trump's brand and name

Donald Trump knew all of this when he decided to put his name on a hotel project in Toronto that was being developed by two immigrants from Russia. Together, they were taking full advantage of Canada's lack of protection for small investors.

Trump was happy to charge his Toronto partners high fees for the use of his brand and his name, for his personal promotion of the sale of the condo units, and for the hotel management services that would be provided by his company.

Trump would take all the credit publicly, but deny any liability for the inevitable disaster for the inexperienced investors who risked their life savings – their family homes – to invest in a project in which Donald Trump promised them a return as solid as a bond.

There were no warnings in the sales campaign about the significant risks. The sales documents were woefully incomplete and misleading. There was no disclosure of the tough reality of the hotel business. **There was no admission that it would take five years for the hotel to become profitable.** There was no "leadership" from Mr. Trump advising potential investors on their need to have other assets and sources of income to cover recessionary business cycles when the hotel's profitability is flat or declining.

With his usual bluster and bravado, Trump dazzled middle-class investors with the attractive aspects of the Trump International Hotel in Toronto.

In a promotional clip posted on YouTube, Donald Trump said of his Toronto project:

"To purchase an apartment or a hotel suite is something very special. I would view this as one of the really good investments. I won't put my name on any building unless it's the best. I have a brand and a name that's the most important thing I have."

In fact, Trump's name and brand have not produced a successful business.

The Trump International Hotel in Toronto is such an economic disaster that all of the small investors who bought individual suites are not the only losers.

Trump's Russian-Canadian partners are desperate to have his name removed from the project in order to cut their huge losses and allow an untainted brand to take over.

3 – The Deceptive Pitch

It is easy to see why potential investors were taken in by Donald Trump's sales pitch. To the unsophisticated investor, the commercial core of Toronto looks like an ideal place to make money owning a hotel suite.

Toronto is the 4th most populous city in North America – larger than Chicago, Houston, or Atlanta. More than 6-millon live in the Toronto metropolitan area – about 17% of the entire 35-million people of Canada (a nation that has almost the same population as California).

Compared to the continent's sprawling giants – Mexico City, New York City, and Los Angeles – Toronto is miraculously safe and clean, and easy to navigate. Tourism and corporate activity attract thousands of people to Toronto year-round, and they need overnight accommodation, particularly in the downtown core.

Toronto is the business capital of Canada, teeming with head-offices filled with bankers, financiers, stock brokers, and deal-makers of all descriptions. Business travellers flock to Toronto from everywhere in Canada and every part of the globe.

Toronto is home to Canada's only teams in Major League Baseball and the National Basketball Association. Moreover, the Toronto Blue Jays and the Toronto Raptors are championship contenders who routinely draw full houses to their stadiums.

Hockey is Canada's national obsession – so much so that the Toronto Maple Leafs sell out every seat for every game in their large new arena, even though they have not won the Stanley Cup since 1967.

The world's most popular game, soccer, has taken solid root in a city of immigrants from around the world, so there are continual expansions of the home stadium of the Toronto Football Club.

All of these games are played in the city's core, which also hosts world-class live entertainment of every description.

The Blue Jays' stadium is one of the engineering marvels of the world with its fully-retractable roof providing reliable conditions at any time of year.

The adjacent CN Tower, which held bragging rights for many years as the world's tallest freestanding structure, continues to be the highest in the western hemisphere. It still draws millions of visitors (similar to the Empire State Building in New York) 40 years after it was built. Far from being a tourist trap, the revolving restaurant combines decent food at reasonable prices with the spectacular views – which include the clouds of mist that rise from Niagara Falls about 40 miles in the distance across massive Lake Ontario.

Every weekend, the highways around Toronto are notable for the many U.S. licence plates on the inbound cars.

It is a tradition for many of the 29-million Canadians who don't live in Toronto to visit the safe and clean Big City periodically to take in a game or a show.

Toronto is a compulsory stop for almost every foreign tour group, especially because of the convenient proximity of Niagara Falls – an easy day trip by bus or train for visitors based in a Toronto hotel.

Toronto *should* be a great place to invest in a hotel, but there's a significant problem that Donald Trump had to know, but did not reveal to the eager investors he was wooing.

Too much competition

The problem for investors is that Toronto has plenty of hotel rooms, and there are no significant barriers to entry for providers of additional suites. Individuals who are marketing directly on the internet are everywhere, and the supply of new hotels exceeds the potential demand except for the rare occasions when there is a large convention in the city.

Even when Toronto hosted the Pan American Games in 2015, there was no shortage of hotel rooms.

Toronto City Council caters to the tourism industry, and welcomes new hotel developments.

For example, within steps of the baseball, basketball, and hockey stadiums is a new 46-storey hotel tower with 567 luxury suites operated under the well-known Canadian brand Delta, a subsidiary of Marriott. Most of the rooms have good views in a bright and airy part of the city core. It's Marriott quality at affordable prices (in the range of $200 a night).

That new hotel is in the sweet spot for Canadian travellers, who are loathe to pay luxury prices except for a once-in-a-lifetime splurge. Canada is dominated by a frugal middle class – and there is only a tiny percentage of truly wealthy people who can afford rooms at Trump rates.

Moreover, at the same time as Trump was selling condo-hotel suites in Toronto that would rely on a nightly rate over $500, three world-class luxury hotels were nearing completion in the same market under brands that assure luxurious quality with understated elegance. Shangri-la, Ritz-Carlton, and Four Seasons are brands that the truly wealthy know and trust.

Particularly, Four Seasons is the first choice for people with real money. The world's leading chain of luxury hotels was founded in Toronto, and its flagship hotel is clearly the best in the city.

As well as these top-brand giants, Toronto also has superb boutique hotels, and impressive offerings from every other brand – all in the same bustling, but safe and clean, downtown core.

If a sophisticated investor such as a pension fund considered putting money into a hotel project in Toronto, it would first conduct a thorough market study of supply and demand. If Donald Trump undertook a market study in Toronto, he kept the results to himself, because such essential information was not provided to the 206 vulnerable investors who were convinced by his sales pitch to give Mr. Trump's Toronto partners deposits in the range of $200,000.

Ignoring the basic principles

Location and appealing to repeat customers are the keys to success in the hotel industry.

Trump's Toronto hotel has locational **dis**advantages in the highly competitive market.

It is not connected to Toronto's extensive and popular PATH system, which provides indoor links to most of the downtown office towers, shopping, and attractions, as well as to the clean and efficient subway system. During the long Canadian winter, and at other times of extreme weather, there is a huge advantage in being able to do business, dine, and attend attractions in climate-controlled comfort. Trump has thus hosted many first-time guests who vow to stay at a PATH-connected hotel the next time they are in Toronto.

Despite being a few blocks from scenic Lake Ontario, Trump's hotel has few rooms with attractive views. The hotel suites are in the bottom half of a tower that is surrounded by office towers.

Trump's hotel is located in a rather dark canyon of high-density urban development.

Regular visits by business travellers are essential for city-core hotels to thrive, but Trump's Toronto property not only lacks indoor access to the nearby office towers, but also competes poorly because of high rates, and the lack of convenience facilities in the rooms. Business travellers staying for several nights appreciate kitchenettes, for example, which Trump does not provide.

Certainly there are plenty of Canadians who will try Trump once – but that cannot provide a sustainable economic base for the hotel business. Moreover, most Canadians will be enticed to a hotel like Trump's only if they can grab a bargain rate offered on the internet.

The only advantage offered to investors by Donald Trump was the Trump name, and it has failed to drive the level of rate and occupancy required to make the hotel a success.

Planning to make their money up-front

Donald Trump was the public face of the marketing program for condominium units that formed the basis for financing the hotel. He promoted the project as if it were another Trump hotel like all the others, and that investors would have a consistent, ongoing, close relationship with Donald Trump himself.

In fact, Trump and his developer-partners never intended to leave any of their own money invested in a hotel business in Toronto.

Their scheme was to be financed not only by the sale of residential condos on top of the hotel portion of the tower (which is common in other projects featuring branded hotels), but also by selling the hotel rooms as condominium units to be owned by individual investors.

20

Their intention was to make their profits upfront by selling *all* of the real estate as condo-hotel suites and luxury apartments, and then continue to profit through charging fees to manage the hotel and its bars and restaurants on behalf of the condo corporation that would represent the individual investor-owners.

Potential investors were lured to buy the condo units by advertising materials that featured Donald Trump front and center.

Even the telephone number for would-be investors anywhere in North America featured the name of the man who was responsible for convincing the buyers: 1-866-91-TRUMP.

"Owning a bond you can sleep in"

The most compelling enticement was a full-page magazine advertisement headlined "Owning a bond you can sleep in" – copies of which were presented to prospective investors at the glamorous sales center at the Toronto site.

It features Trump and Dr. Stephen Soloway, described as a "New Jersey rheumatologist" who has "sterling credentials" in both medicine and real estate.

"Philadelphia Magazine rates him as one of the best physicians in the United States. On the real estate side, he has made a fortune as an investor, mainly through the purchase of condominium hotel suites. 'It's like owning a bond you can sleep in'.

"When he heard that the Trump Organization and its partner, Talon International Development Inc., were creating a magnificent 60-storey residential and luxury hotel tower in Toronto, he was among the first to invest. He bought a pair of two-bedroom residential suites plus three studio hotel condominiums.

"His plan is to let the Trump Organization manage them, renting both residential and hotel suites while he earns a satisfying return on his money. …

"Dr. Soloway has words of advice for would-be real-estate investors. 'If you are going to invest, invest in the best. The market will always be there. With those Trump Towers, I believe you can count on it.' "

Investors were promised "great cash flows, no concerns for maintenance, and reasonable cash requirements as a down payment. Leverage is key, especially in these times of low interest rates."

Based on that pitch, Trump's sales agents enthusiastically prepared a customized "Estimated Return on Investment" spreadsheet for each condo unit that caught the attention of any potential investor who ventured into the sales center.

Investors were told that it would be easy to obtain a mortgage for 65% of the purchase price, and they were shown how much return to expect on the 35% cash that they would be investing. Purchase prices started at about $800,000 (Canadian funds) for 500 sq.ft.

In fact, it was impossible to obtain that much financing from banks or other mainstream lenders. The 50 victimized investors did not learn until it was too late that the bankers knew it was a bad investment.

Sadly, they allowed themselves to be *leveraged* into a destructive financial trap.

For a prominent New Jersey doctor, investing in property
at Toronto's new Trump International Hotel & Tower is like...

OWNING A BOND YOU CAN SLEEP IN.

Dr. Stephen Soloway readily agrees that he has two passions in life: medicine and real estate. The New Jersey rheumatologist has sterling credentials in both fields.

Philadelphia Magazine rates him as one of the best physicians in the United States. On the real estate side, he has made a fortune as an investor, mainly through his purchase of condominium hotel suites.

"It's like owning a bond you can sleep in," he says.

When he heard the Trump Organization and its partner, Talon International Development Inc. were creating a magnificent 60-storey residential and luxury hotel tower in Toronto, he was among the first to invest. He bought a pair of two-bedroom residential suites plus three studio hotel condominiums.

His plan is to let the Trump Organization manage them, renting both residential and hotel suites while he earns a satisfying return on his money.

Investing in hotel suites is a trend sweeping the United States, says CNNMoney.com, the news network's on-line magazine. The reason? Great cash flows, no concerns for maintenance and reasonable cash requirements as a down payment. Leverage is key, especially in these times of low interest rates.

"I love the Trump properties and I own suites in four of them," says Dr. Soloway. In fact, he has five suites in New York, three in Chicago, five in Las Vegas and five in Toronto. The doctor also owns suites in other hotel properties throughout the United States. Toronto's Trump International Hotel & Tower, however, holds a special place in his heart.

"Toronto is a wonderful city and it has emerged as a major world centre for arts, entertainment, sports and investment. Just look at the flow of US and

Donald Trump (left) and Dr. Stephen Soloway are equally enthusiastic about Trump Toronto.

European and even Asian investors eager to cash in on its real estate," he says.

"These suites allow small investors like me to do the same thing. My philosophy is to do what feels right," he says. "I would never buy anything I could not live in myself and I focus on five-star properties. They are virtually recession proof."

As Dr. Soloway points out, no matter what direction the economy turns, wealthy people will always travel and they will always stay at the best hotel cities have to offer. The new Toronto Trump International Hotel & Tower, situated in the heart of the financial district at Bay and Adelaide streets will be the one of the very few world class five-star properties. It is certain to draw athletes, celebrities, top business executives, in fact, anyone with a longing for luxury, Dr. Soloway says.

His view is that those same factors apply to Trump Tower residences.

The two residences he has purchased, both two-bedroom suites, will sit high up in the tower. "I chose one looking north and one looking south over the lake," Dr. Soloway says. "That way I have both of those splendid views covered."

Dr. Soloway says he bought the New York City Trump International suites right after 9/11, an enormously clever move as it turned out.

"When that tower was built in 1997 it sold for $US500 a square foot. Just before 9/11, the asking prices were in the $US2,000 to $US2,500 a foot range," he says. "The

events of 9/11 drove prices down to about $1,000 a foot and that is when I jumped in. I knew the property would come back and it has."

Trump New York is running at an 83% occupancy rate, which means Dr. Soloway collects his share of room rents much like an annuity.

"The cash flow has been tremendous; it allowed me to reinvest in those other properties in Chicago, Las Vegas and Toronto," he says.

Toronto has also provided him with another unexpected return. He bought his five suites when the Canadian dollar was valued at just 73 cents US. Its recent rise has not changed his mind about the value of Trump Toronto, however.

"I got in when prices were about $600 a foot, I would guess prices are about $1,200 a foot or so right now. I can easily see them rising to $1,800 or even $2,000 a foot by the time the tower is completed or shortly thereafter," Dr. Soloway says.

With construction now well underway, a limited selection of the property's most popular executive-sized residential suites have recently been released for sale. Prices start at a reasonable CAD$1.8-million.

Dr. Soloway has words of advice for would-be real estate investors.

"If you are going to invest, invest in the best," he says. "The market will always be there. With those Trump Towers I believe you can count on it."

Sales are by appointment only. The presentation centre is located at 120 Adelaide Street West, Suite 110, Toronto, ON Canada, and the telephone number is +1 416-214-2800 or toll free in North America at 1-866-91 TRUMP. The web address is www.trumptoronto.ca/bizlife ■

"My philosophy is to do what feels right."
— Dr. Stephen Soloway

4 – "No possible profit"

With a grand show of personal fanfare, Donald Trump presided at the ground-breaking in Toronto in 2007. By the time the overdue project finally welcomed its first paying guest in January 2012, it was deeply mired in complaints of investor fraud and low demand for occupancy.

Trump's developer-partners are currently stuck with millions worth of unsold condos, and the 50 individuals who were deceived into carrying on with their investments in the hotel-condo units are each out of pocket by hundreds of thousands of Canadian dollars.

In *Singh v. Trump*, judge Paul Perell exonerated Donald Trump in a manner that is typical of the way Canadian courts protect rich, important, and powerful people.

At paragraph 31 of his decision, the judge acknowledged that Mr. Trump had been seen by the investors as an "icon"; that his name is a "brand"; and that his association with the hotel caused a "buzz" of interest. However, the court absolved Trump of any *personal* liability because all actions were taken by corporations and through the use of licences between corporations, and not, as a matter of civil law in Canada, by Trump personally.

"Just having one's name associated with a development project does not establish the degree of proximity required to give rise to a duty of care to investors in that development project." (Para. 34)

"Proximity" is an important concept in Canadian civil law, because it allows individuals to escape personal liability through the use of corporations and licence agreements to reduce their "proximity".

Judge Perell ruled against the plaintiffs on every claim, citing Canadian civil law that provides very little protection to consumers –

especially because vendors can escape liability for false advertising by inserting "exculpatory" clauses into the final sales contracts.

Judges believe that such clauses wipe out any civil liability for promises made before the final legal contract is signed, unless they are contained within that final contract. They overlook the fact that money has been taken and held by the seller as deposits based on the original oral contracts. Judges allow the sellers like Trump and his corporate partners to escape liability *retroactively* by burying escape clauses in thick, dense final contracts.

Perell stated that the individual investors should have known it would be unreasonable to rely on the misleading marketing materials – which were presented in the name of Donald Trump.

Deceptive documents based on "guesswork"

Judge Perell was blunt in his description of the "Estimates" that had been provided to each of the investors (and reproduced at para. 64 of the ruling), which typically suggested returns on cash invested ranging from 7% to 20% (based on hotel occupancies ranging from 55% to 75%):

"The Estimates were replete with misrepresentations of commission, of omission, and of half-truth. The Estimates were deceptive documents." (Para. 212 of *Singh v. Trump*)

In his campaign for President, Trump proposes to replace "political hacks" with his own team of business-minded managers to run the federal government. His choice of executive partners in Toronto is revealing.

Judge Perell described the Estimates as nothing more than "guesswork", produced by the CEO of the Toronto-based development company, a Russian émigré named Val Levitan. The

Estimates were based on fees and expenses that were either significantly understated or not disclosed at all to the investors.

"Mr. Levitan prepared the Estimates that are at the heart of this litigation. He is not an accountant and does not have experience in construction, hotel management, or operations." (Para. 36)

"Mr. Levitan had no training, experience, or justification from actual research to make any projections about the revenue streams for the new hotel in Toronto. What actually happened shows how inaccurate Mr. Levitan's guesswork was." (Para. 215)

The Canadian judge particularly cited the $48-a-night reservation fee, the existence of which had not been disclosed to the investors until after the hotel started operating. This fee for running the reservation system was taken off the top of any hotel rental by Trump, in addition to other management fees charged to owners by Trump. "With occupancy rates in the 50% range, there is no possible profit with this reservation free." (Para. 218)

Most of the purchasers were told that they would be able to finance their purchases with mortgages for 65% of the total price, and that they would have to pay only 35% of that price in order to become investor-owners in the Trump hotel. For reasons that are not explained, plaintiff Singh was told he needed to deposit only 25% of the purchase price upfront, and that he could obtain a mortgage for the remaining 75% of the total capital cost of $804,000 by mortgage. Singh was also not told that the actual purchase price would be $869,000. (Para. 67)

Here are the yearly costs provided to plaintiff Singh in the **Estimated Return on Investment** document that persuaded him to commit to pay $201,000 as a deposit on a condo-hotel suite priced at $804,000, with the expectation that the hotel would have 75% occupancy and his suite would earn an average of $550 per night from paying guests:

$21,900 for "common expense fees" (typically known as condo fees)

$16,425 for "occupancy fees" (housekeeping services)

$16,080 for "estimated property taxes" (payable to City of Toronto)

$46,621.55 for mortgage payments at 6% rate of interest

$101,026.55 total expenses

$150,562.50 revenue from suite rental

$49,535.95 yearly return (revenue over expenses)

24.64% return on $201,000 cash invested

When the hotel started serving guests in 2012, Mr. Singh's suite had an average nightly rental rate of $427.88 (not $550) and the occupancy was only 33.2% (not 75%). There was no payment to Mr. Singh for net hotel income, because there was none after all the fees and charges were deducted. Instead, he received a bill for monthly fees that he would have to pay regardless of the income, if any, that the hotel might be earning on his suite. (Para. 158 of *Singh v. Trump*)

What this bill disclosed was that the following costs had increased (reported by the judge on a monthly basis, but calculated by this author on an annual basis for comparison to the costs cited above in the Estimated Return on Investment):

$35,183 for "common expense fees" (condo fees) – an increase from $21,900

$28,677 for "estimated property taxes" (City of Toronto) – up from $16,080

This bill also disclosed a significant new cost for Mr. Singh (again calculated on an annual basis for comparison):

$11,466 for sales taxes payable to the provincial and federal governments

These three items increased the total of expenses by $37,346, eliminating 75% of the "Estimate" of $49,535.95 yearly return (revenue over expenses) dangled in front of Mr. Singh in the deceptive sales document. But, there was much worse to come in terms of undisclosed costs and fees that would eliminate all possible profit and create substantial losses that Mr. Singh and the 49 other victims would have to pay on a continuing basis.

In paragraph 167, Judge Perell listed two more previously-undisclosed fees:

3 to 3.25% of hotel suite revenue as a management fee

2% of hotel suite revenue for a reserve fund in 2013 (increasing to **3%** in 2014 and **4%** in 2015)

As well, there were **increases in the nightly charge for housekeeping services** that were not specified by the judge.

In paragraph 169, Perell reported on the final undisclosed new charge payable to the Trump management:

$48 per night for reservation services

That is the fee that prompted the judge to determine that there was no possibility of investors making a profit.

Certainty of early losses not disclosed

"The Estimates make no mention of the fact that, like every business, early losses at the hotel could be expected while the hotel built up its goodwill and its trade and commerce." (Para. 216 of *Singh v. Trump*)

At a meeting of owner-investors on Oct. 24, 2013, the management finally disclosed that "it would take time for the hotel to become profitable, approximately five years." (Para. 194)

Judge Perell continued: "The Estimates' specification of expenses was erroneous. Three of the four expenses ... were understated, two of them significantly. In addition, five other material and inevitable expenses were not disclosed." (Para. 217)

One of those undisclosed fees alone was enough to ensure that the investment would become a liability:

"The omission of the reservation fee of $48 [per night] is telling. It amounts to about 16% of the actual nightly room rates charged at the hotel, and with occupancy rates in the 50% range, there is no profit possible with this reservation fee." (Para. 218)

The judge listed the increased and added expenses, but did not total them. It is clear that the expenses greatly exceed the potential revenue – even with the impossibly-high nightly rates and occupancy percentages promised in the Trump marketing plan.

After the hotel opened, the investors were paying more to the management of the Trump International Hotel for their share of expenses than they were earning as their share of hotel revenue. The plaintiffs were losing $4,000 to $5,000 per month – forcing them to pay more *into* the hotel business instead of receiving the profits shown in the Estimate.

Thus, they had no funds from their investment to make payments on the loans they had taken out for the purchase deposits and to finance the full price on closing.

Singh was never able to obtain mortgage financing and was not able to close the purchase, thus losing his purchase deposits that had come to $173,400 by that point.

This was money that he had borrowed from his father, a retired welder, who had in turn borrowed the money by taking out a line of credit secured against the family home.

In paragraph 193, Judge Perell itemized the Singh claim as of Dec. 31, 2014, but totally dismissed it:

$173,400.00   Deposit

$ 29,113.62   Loss during Interim Occupancy

$ 45,550.96   Interest Paid to his Father

$248,064.58   Total Loss

In addition to this total, Singh would have had to pay his own two lawyers, plus the legal costs of the winning side. Trump and his partners had two lawyers fighting Singh and Lee (and the other 48 investors who would have benefited if Singh and Lee had won).

Judge Perell ordered Singh and Lee, the two plaintiffs, to pay Donald Trump and his development partners a total of $58,000 for their lawyer costs. Assuming that Singh paid half of this, his total loss came to $277,064.58 for investing in a "bond that you can sleep in".

How close to worthless are these hotel suites?

The other plaintiff in the test case before Judge Perell, Ms. Lee, had been able to borrow only $300,000 from a bank for a condo mortgage. She had paid $157,000 in deposits, and raised the rest by borrowing $400,000 against the family home. Ms. Lee thus completed the purchase of her hotel suite at the end of November 2012, and continued to endure losses.

At paragraph 195 of his decision, Perell stated that Ms. Lee had endured operating losses from October 2012 to December 2014 that totalled $134,576.92.

He then stated that her total losses at the end of 2014 came to $991,576.92, based on the judge's assumption that her condo-hotel suite for which she had paid $857,000 was now unsaleable.

While it is unlikely that such a piece of condominium real estate in the core of Toronto is totally worthless, the fact remains that there will be no realistic market for any of the hotel suites (or the private residential apartments in the tower above the Trump International Hotel) until there is a new owner of the project who has deep enough pockets to clean up the mess and re-brand it as something more palatable than Trump.

Again the question arises as to why Mr. Trump himself, if he is so immensely wealthy and so confident of his ability to make profits in the hotel business – and so concerned about protecting his name and his brand, did not simply repay the investors and own all the suites himself.

There is no evidence that Donald Trump or any of his corporations ever owned any of the suites in the Trump International Hotel in Toronto. They were all initially owned by Talon International Development Inc., the corporation controlled by Trump's Russian-Canadian partners, who had managed to sell some of the condo-hotel suites to the losing investors.

Most of those investors were middle-class people with modest means and very little investment experience. They relied on the assurances and reputation of Donald Trump, and they suffered devastating losses.

"To purchase an apartment or a hotel suite is something very special. I would view this as one of the really good investments," Trump said in a promotional clip (posted on YouTube on July 24, 2008).

"I won't put my name on any building unless it's the best. I have a brand and a name that's the most important thing I have."

Developers stuck with unsold condos

Trump's developer-partners in Toronto had taken deposits for 206 condo-hotel units, but only 50 purchasers ultimately closed their transactions. (Para. 189)

The other 156 investors had better lawyers than Singh and Lee. Under Canadian law – which is not easy for the average investor to understand – the construction delays had created an opportunity to withdraw from the transaction before closing. However, the investors had to have expert legal advice to learn this and act upon it in order to recover much of their money, because they were not told by Trump's marketing agents that they had a right to withdraw.

All of those 156 investors endured losses, but much less than the 50 who did not have lawyers who knew how to escape from a deteriorating investment that was not being completed according to the terms of the sales contracts.

Of the total of 261 hotel-condo units, Trump's developer-partners still owned 209 when they won the lawsuit in 2015. However, they had already stopped trying to sell any more units.

There were plenty of warnings showing up in the mainstream news media as well as in internet blogs.

By that time, every real-estate agent in Toronto knew that the Trump International Hotel was a losing proposition with no hope of recovery, and no agent would risk his or her reputation by advising a client to buy a condo unit under the Trump brand.

Above the hotel portion of the tower are 118 larger residential condos, of which only about half were sold to individuals. Some of the buyers intended to use them as full-time residences, while others were investors expecting rental income through Trump's promotion and management.

It is unusual for any condo developer to be stuck with so much inventory, and Trump's developer-partners are looking for an exit, believing that Trump's tarnished reputation is making it impossible to sell suites to individuals.

The most likely escape for the Toronto developer-partners is a bulk sale to a deep-pocketed corporation that would rebrand the hotel and start fresh.

In December 2015, Trump's lawyers filed a lawsuit in Toronto aimed to prevent his partners from terminating the hotel management contract and removing Trump's name from the building.

The Toronto Globe and Mail quoted Symon Zucker, a lawyer for Trump's Toronto partners at Talon International Developments: "They're not happy with us, but mostly we're not happy with Donald."

5 – What's in a Name?

Talon, *noun*, the claw of a bird of prey.

Mark, *noun*, an object of attack, ridicule or abuse; a victim of a swindle.

Trump and his partners created several corporations to execute their Trump International Hotel project in Canada. Their choice of corporate names falls into the category of unintentional satire.

The promoters and developers literally sank their talons into the marks.

Alex Shnaider and Val Levitan, two Russian-Canadians, formed **Talon International Development Inc.** to undertake the hotel development in partnership with Trump Toronto Hotel Management Corp., which they contracted to manage and market the hotel (including the reservations system), and operate the housekeeping service.

The Trump Organization created **Trump Marks Toronto LP** to licence the Trump trademark to Talon, which used the Trump brand to sell condo units.

More than half of the people of Toronto are non-European minorities for whom English is unlikely to be the family's first language. The unintended revelation in the meanings of the words Mark and Talon would have been lost on them.

Shnaider made his original fortune in Russia during the period after the fall of communism. (He continues as the principal in Talon, but has replaced Levitan with a professional hotel manager.)

If, instead of Donald Trump, Shnaider had been the public face of the project, his reputation as an aggressive Russian businessman might have warned the prospective purchasers to be wary of buying condos from Talon International Development Inc.

6 – "Deceit, Falsehood or other Fraudulent Means"

It is ironic that Donald Trump's development partners in Toronto are Russian immigrants.

There is a well-known Russian proverb that applies well to this situation in Canada. It is usually quoted in English this way:

Little thieves are hanged, but great ones escape.

The direct translation is:

The thief who stole an altyn (3 kopecks) is hung, and the one who stole a poltinnik (50 kopecks) is praised.

It should be no surprise to anyone familiar with the attitude of most Canadian prosecutors and judges that Donald Trump was never at risk of being held liable in a civil lawsuit in Canada, let alone being charged with the criminal offence of fraud for his role in the Toronto Trump Tower – because of the way the law is wrongly interpreted by Canadian courts.

Because the likelihood of conviction is so low, there is little effort by the police to investigate corporate crime. Canada's national police force, the Royal Canadian Mounted Police (the equivalent of the FBI), was notorious for its low priority on fraud charges. For Canada's largest province (Ontario, with 14-million of Canada's total of 36-million people), the RCMP dedicated only two officers to review complaints from citizens about white-collar crime.

Large-scale fraud is a serious problem in Canada. Despite the fact that the Criminal Code of Canada sets out a very clear definition of fraud (see below), few charges have ever been laid against rich, important, and powerful people doing business improperly in Canada.   In several of the few high-profile cases where charges have been laid, Canadian courts found the defendants not guilty.

It is extremely rare for a major corporate fraud to result in prison sentences for the culprits. One exception was the case of Garth Drabinsky and Myron Gottlieb, the founders and top executives of Livent, which was a major producer of Broadway musicals and the proprietor of live theatres in New York, Toronto, and other major cities in North America from 1990 to 1998.

Prosecutors in the United States shamed Canadian officials into taking action. But, even in this case, they dilly-dallied for a decade before bringing a whittled-down case to trial – and the Canadian courts were shockingly lenient.

Livent's apparent success, which conned investors into buying high-priced shares in the publicly-traded company, was based on fraudulent accounting. Expenses were hidden or improperly reported.   Ticket revenues were overstated, including a scheme by which an associate of the company bought full-price tickets by the hundred (even though no one actually attended) and was then reimbursed as payment for engineering or other services (which were then reported as capital assets instead of operating losses).

As well, the founders arranged large kickbacks for themselves to get around bankers' limits on how much they could be paid for their personal contributions to the corporation.

The founders were seen living the high life to an extreme, which added to their false image of success in producing Broadway musicals with big box-office revenues and fat profits.

The money received from the sale of shares was used to cover the hidden losses, as well as the founders' luxurious lifestyle.

The scammers eventually ran out of money, and had to seek deep-pocketed investors to take over their assets. The American businessmen who bought Livent for its theatres and the production rights to the ongoing shows discovered the massive fraud. Broadway musicals that were reported to shareholders as profitable were actually running at a loss and had to be shut down.

In January 1999, U.S. authorities in New York laid a large number of criminal and civil charges against the corporation and its executives, mainly against Drabinsky and Gottlieb. Canada's Financial Post newspaper estimated that the two men faced possible penalties totaling 140 years in prison plus $16-million in fines for their roles in a fraud that CNN estimated had cost shareholders $100-million.

Drabinsky and Gottlieb refused to leave Canada to face the charges in the U.S. – and Canadian authorities allowed them to remain in Canada despite being fugitives.

It took 2.5 years for Canadian authorities to lay charges, and another 7 years to actually bring the case to trial in Toronto.

By the time the case was placed in front of a Canadian judge in 2008, only three charges were presented. Drabinsky and Gottlieb were staunchly supported by leading members of the Canadian establishment, who played down the significance of accounting fraud that Canadian prosecutors were now saying had cost the shareholders $500-million.

Most observers were surprised when the two men were actually convicted of fraud and forgery. Drabinsky was sentenced to 7 years in prison, while number-two executive Gottlieb was sentenced to 6 years. No fines were levied.

The Ontario Court of Appeal upheld the convictions, but reduced the sentences to 5 years and 4 years. Because most criminals are eligible for parole in Canada after serving only one-third of their sentences, the penalties were very small by U.S. standards.

(Drabinsky was in prison for approximately 17 months before being granted day parole. He was then allowed to live an almost-normal life in a "half-way house" for a further 11 months before being granted full parole.)

The reason given by the Court of Appeal for reducing the sentence is typical of the attitude taken by Canadian judges in dealing with corporate fraud. <u>The Court of Appeal actually said that there was no evidence of any financial loss</u> caused by the fraudulent practices of Drabinsky and Gottlieb, and therefore the trial judge erred by setting the sentences too high.

The message from the Canadian courts is depressingly clear: It's **buyer beware** in any investment.

What the law says – and how it was wrongly interpreted

What follows are exact reproductions of the relevant sections of the Criminal Code of Canada.

What is most shocking about what the law says and how it is interpreted is in section 380.1(1)(d), which provides for *additional* punishment ("aggravating circumstance") when the offender takes advantage of the high regard in which the offender is held in the community.

In fact, as can be seen by the lenient manner in which Drabinsky and Gottlieb were sentenced, the court reversed the intent of the law: The culprits were let off easily because of their stature and the support they received from so many high-placed persons – yet it was the fact they were held in such high regard that made it possible for them to run their fraud for so long without attracting appropriate scrutiny.

Note also that it is an "aggravating circumstance" when the fraud has a large number of victims, which is the case for a publicly-traded corporation such as Livent, which had thousands of shareholders.

Note as well that $1-million is set as the threshold for large-scale fraud, and the Livent shareholders' losses were many times in excess of that amount. By any honest assessment of the scale of the fraud committed by Drabinsky and Gottlieb, their prison sentences should have been much closer to the maximum of 14 years each.

Finally, note section 380.1(1)(e). Drabinksy practised law before going into the entertainment business. Because he was educated in the law, and experienced in its interpretation, he should have been subject to a stiffer penalty than a businessman who had not been subject to professional standards.

Criminal Code of Canada: Fraud

380 (1) Every one who, by deceit, falsehood or other fraudulent means, whether or not it is a false pretence within the meaning of this Act, defrauds the public or any person, whether ascertained or not, of any property, money or valuable security or any service,

(a) is guilty of an indictable offence and liable to a term of imprisonment not exceeding fourteen years, where the subject-matter of the offence is a testamentary instrument or the value of the subject-matter of the offence exceeds five thousand dollars;

Minimum punishment

(1.1) When a person is prosecuted on indictment and convicted of one or more offences referred to in subsection (1), the court that imposes the sentence shall impose a minimum punishment of imprisonment for a term of two years if the total value of the subject-matter of the offences exceeds one million dollars.

Sentencing — aggravating circumstances

380.1 (1) Without limiting the generality of section 718.2, where a court imposes a sentence for an offence referred to in section 380, 382, 382.1 or 400, it shall consider the following as aggravating circumstances:

(a) the magnitude, complexity, duration or degree of planning of the fraud committed was significant; ...

(c) the offence involved a large number of victims;

(c.1) the offence had a significant impact on the victims given their personal circumstances including their age, health and financial situation;

(d) in committing the offence, the offender took advantage of the high regard in which the offender was held in the community;

(e) the offender did not comply with a licensing requirement, or professional standard, that is normally applicable to the activity or conduct that forms the subject-matter of the offence;

Aggravating circumstance — value of the fraud

(1.1) Without limiting the generality of section 718.2, when a court imposes a sentence for an offence referred to in section 382, 382.1 or 400, it shall also consider as an aggravating circumstance the fact that the value of the fraud committed exceeded one million dollars.

Non-mitigating factors

(2) When a court imposes a sentence for an offence referred to in section 380, 382, 382.1 or 400, it shall not consider as mitigating circumstances the offender's employment, employment skills or status or reputation in the community if those circumstances were relevant to, contributed to, or were used in the commission of the offence.

What *should* happen now to Donald Trump

There is no statute of limitations for criminal offences in Canada. There is nothing preventing Canadian prosecutors from laying criminal charges *now* against Donald Trump and his partners.

There is ample evidence to justify a trial in Toronto to formally determine if Trump used deceit, falsehood, and other fraudulent means to convince vulnerable investors to buy condominium units as investments that could not possibly earn the promised profits, and were actually very destructive liabilities.

Such charges should be laid before Americans go to the polls in November.

Notice to readers:

The author's belief that there is sufficient evidence to support charging Donald Trump with criminal fraud is only an opinion or comment. It is not a statement of fact, even though it is based on the author's thorough analysis of the facts of the case.

The only way to determine whether or not a person has committed a crime is through the judicial system. Only if a person has been convicted in court of a crime can that person be said to be a criminal.

www.ingramcontent.com/pod-product-compliance
Lightning Source LLC
Chambersburg PA
CBHW062027280526
45787CB00005B/2239